This Planner Belongs To:

_____

_____

_____

Table of Contents

1. Who to Call

2. Personal Information

3. Documents You Will Need and Location

4. Practical and Pertinent

5. Medical Information

6. Medical Information

7. Wishes in Case I Can't Make Decisions

8. Information about Work/ Business

9. Passwords

10. Information on All My Finances

11. Information about Dependents

12. Information You Will Need About My Pets

13. Social Circle

14. Social Information

15. Property Information

16. Household Information

Table of Contents

18. Dealing with the Bills

19. Dealing with My Stuff

20. Dealing with My Stuff

21. My Idea of Final Arrangements

22. Beneficiary Information

23. Last Thoughts of Life

24. Note to Those Left Behind

25. Regrets and Things that have Bugged Me

26. Proudest Times

27. Lessons Learned

28. Apologies

29. Apologies

30. Aspirations for Others

31. Aspirations for Others

32. Advanced Directives

33. Choices for My Last Days

34. Facts You May Not Have Known

35. Updates

Attorney: _____

_____

Spiritual Leader: _____

_____

_____

Doctors: _____

_____

_____

_____

_____

Family/Friends: _____

_____

_____

_____

_____

_____

_____

_____

Personal Information

Name: _____
_____
_____

Address: _____
_____
_____

Citizenship: _____
_____
_____

Documents You Will Need & Location

Will: _____

Power of Attorney: _____

Advanced Directive: _____

Safe Deposit Box: _____

Financial Planner: _____

Practical and Pertinent

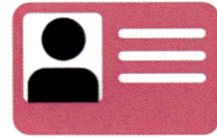

Social Security: _____

_____

Drivers License: _____

_____

Deeds and Titles: _____

_____

_____

Funeral Home: _____

_____

Life Insurance: _____

_____

_____

Auto Insurance: _____

_____

_____

Medical Information

_____

_____

_____

_____

_____

_____

_____

_____

_____

_____

_____

_____

_____

_____

Medical Information

_____

_____

_____

_____

_____

_____

_____

_____

_____

_____

_____

_____

_____

_____

_____

Wishes in Case I Can't Make Decisions

> Death is not the greatest loss in life.
> The greatest loss is what dies inside us
> while we live
>
> ~Norman Cousins

_____
_____
_____
_____
_____
_____
_____
_____
_____
_____
_____
_____

Information About Work/Business

_____

_____

_____

_____

_____

_____

_____

_____

_____

_____

_____

_____

_____

_____

Passwords

_____   _____

_____   _____

_____   _____

_____   _____

_____   _____

_____   _____

_____   _____

_____   _____

_____   _____

_____   _____

_____   _____

_____   _____

Information on My Finances

Information about Dependents

_____

_____

_____

_____

_____

_____

_____

_____

_____

_____

_____

_____

_____

_____

_____

Information You Will Need About My Pets

_____

_____

_____

_____

_____

_____

_____

_____

_____

_____

_____

_____

_____

_____

_____

_____

Social Circle

_____

_____

_____

_____

_____

_____

_____

_____

_____

_____

_____

_____

_____

_____

Social Information

Property Information

_____

_____

_____

_____

_____

_____

_____

_____

_____

_____

_____

_____

_____

_____

_____

_____

Household Information

Dealing with the Bills

Bill	How much?	Which account?

Dealing with My Stuff

_____

_____

_____

_____

_____

_____

_____

_____

_____

_____

_____

_____

_____

_____

_____

_____

_____

_____

Dealing with My Stuff

My Idea of Final Arrangements

Beneficiary Information

Thoughts on this quote:

_____

_____

_____

_____

_____

_____

_____

_____

_____

_____

_____

_____

_____

_____

_____

_____

_____

_____

_____

Last Thoughts of Life

Note to Those Left Behind

Regrets and Things that have Bugged Me

Proudest Times

Career Achievements

_____

_____

_____

_____

_____

_____

_____

_____

_____

_____

_____

_____

_____

_____

_____

Lessons Learned

Apologies

> The darkness of death is like the evening twilight; it makes all objects appear more lovely to the dying.
>
> ~Jean Paul

Apologies

Apologies

Aspirations for Others

Aspirations for Others

Advanced Directives

Choices for my Last Days

Where I want to stay: _____
_____
_____

Company or alone?: _____
_____
_____

Clergy visit?: _____
Who?: _____
_____

Music type/songs?: _____
_____
_____
_____

Facts You May Not Have Known

Favorite movie(s): _____
_____
_____

Favorite actresses: _____
_____

Favorite actors: _____
_____

Favorite books: _____
_____

Favorite authors: _____
_____
_____

Updates

Whatever Life Throws Your Way, Just Remember…

NEVER GIVE UP AND…

Keep on Smiling!

Made in the USA
Las Vegas, NV
29 May 2025